LITTLE SEED

COLORING BOOK

BY KELLEY BROWNE-REYNOLDS

STUDIO
OF BOOKS
THE SPACE FOR YOUR MESSAGE

Studio of Books LLC
5900 Balcones Drive Suite 100
Austin, Texas 78731
www.studioofbooks.org
Hotline: (254) 800-1183

Ordering Information:
Special discounts are available on quantity purchases by corporations, associations, and others. For details, contact the publisher at the address above.

Printed in the United States of America.

ISBN-13: Softcover   978-1-968491-53-6
          eBook   978-1-968491-54-3

Library of Congress Control Number: 2025915435

Little Seed lived in a small tree in

The Big Tree Forest

On a cool night in early spring, a storm rolled in.

Little Seed was plucked from her cozy branch. She

whirled and twirled through the air until…thud!

She landed on the forest floor.

Little Seed looked to the left.

Then looked to

the right.

"Where am I?"

Suddenly, a group of seeds surrounded her.

"Have you ever seen anything like her?"

"Where did she come from?"

She became filled with shame.

"There must be something wrong with me?"

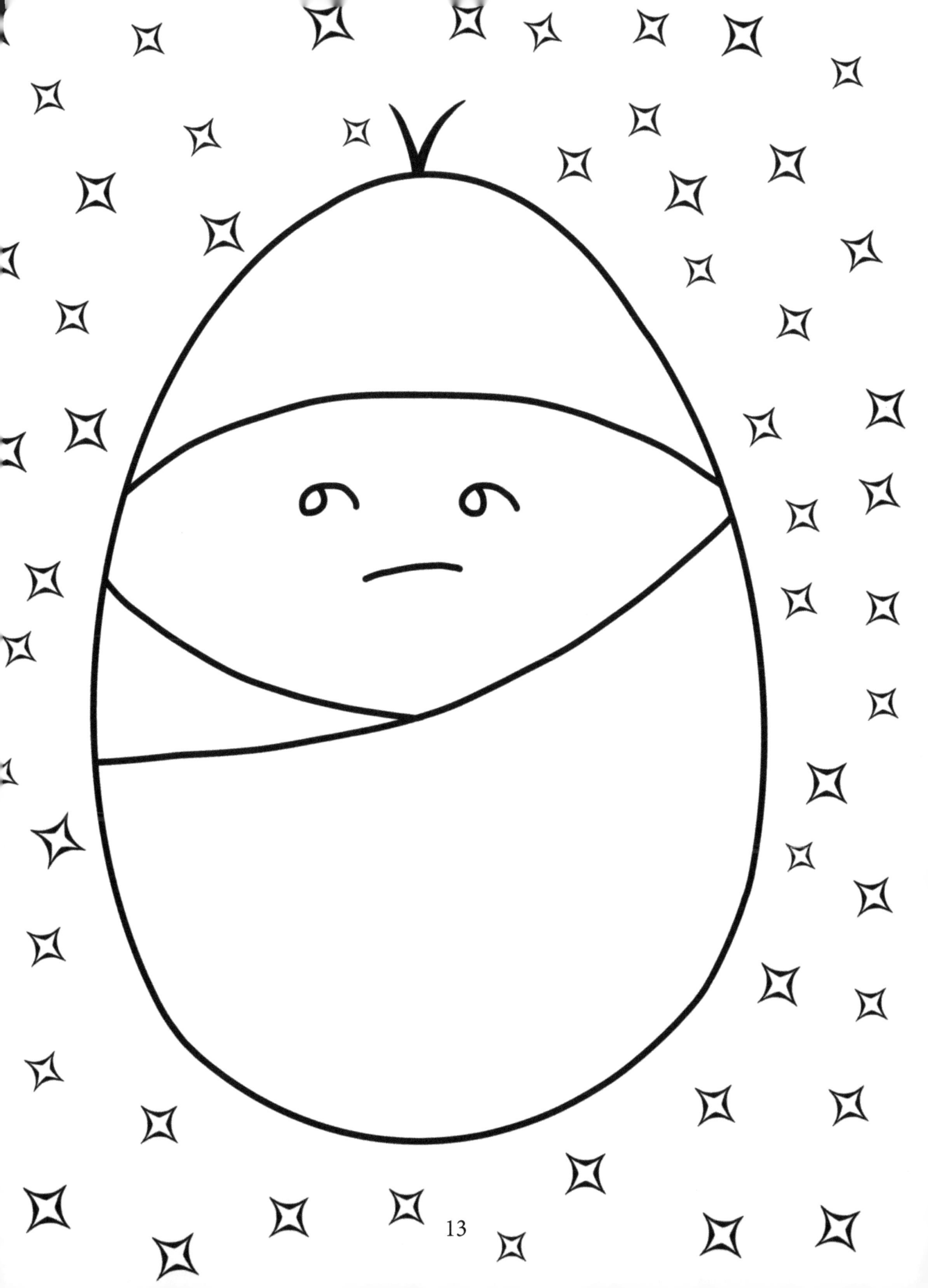

She felt heavy with sadness in this new world.

With nowhere to turn, she allowed herself to sink

into the cold, dark, squishy earth.

Little Seed felt cold and alone.

"I just want to go home!"

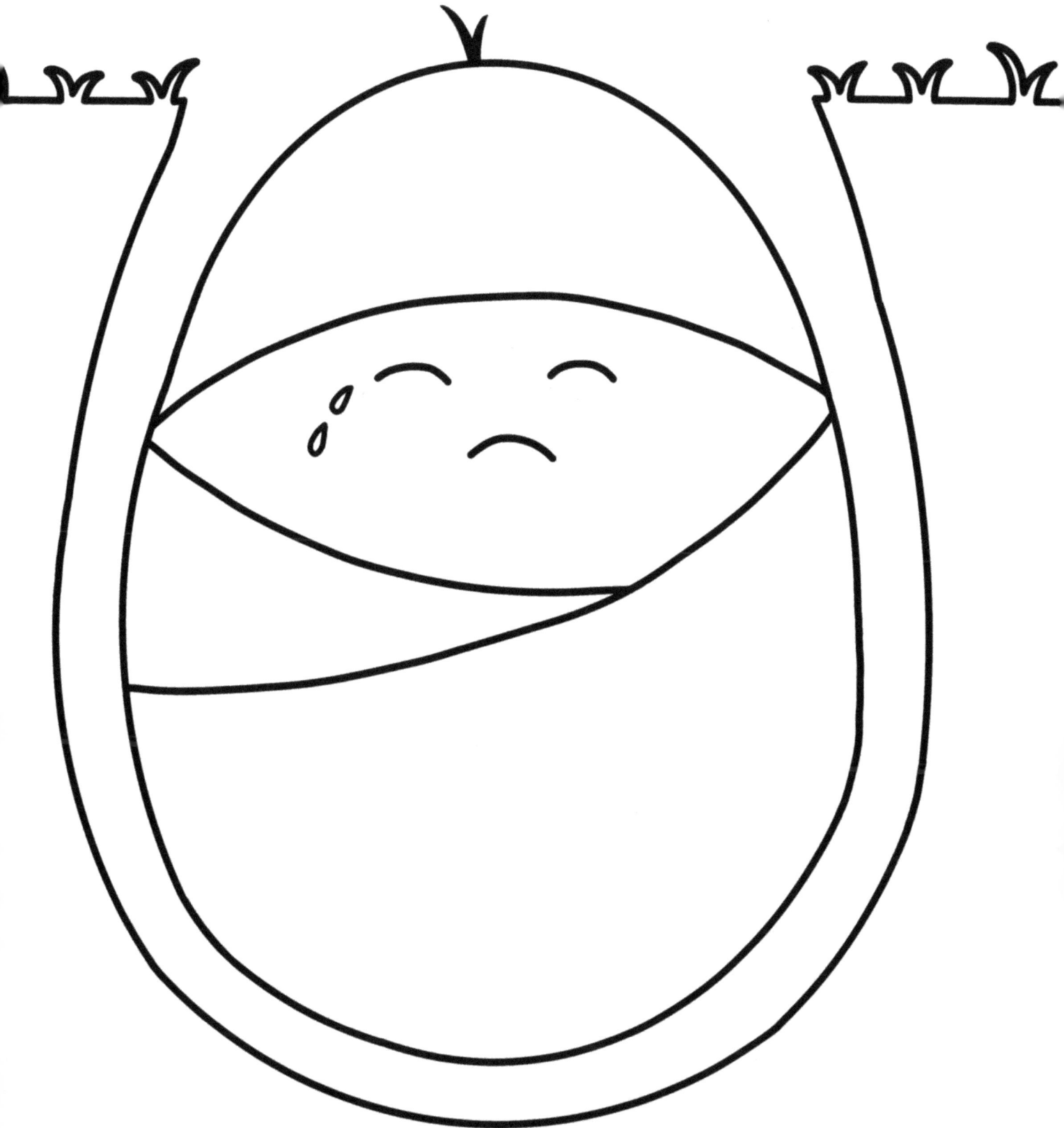

One day, she saw a worm approaching.

"Stay away, no one likes me!"

"Why would you say that?", asked The Worm

"Because that's how the other seeds

made me feel."

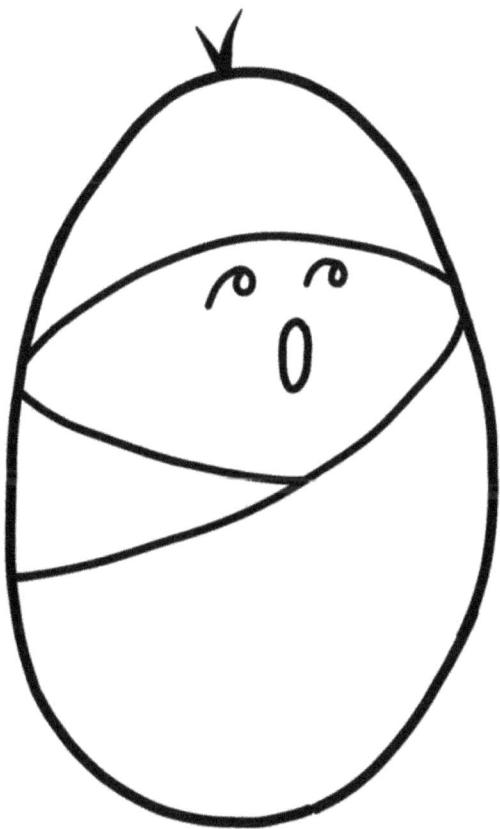
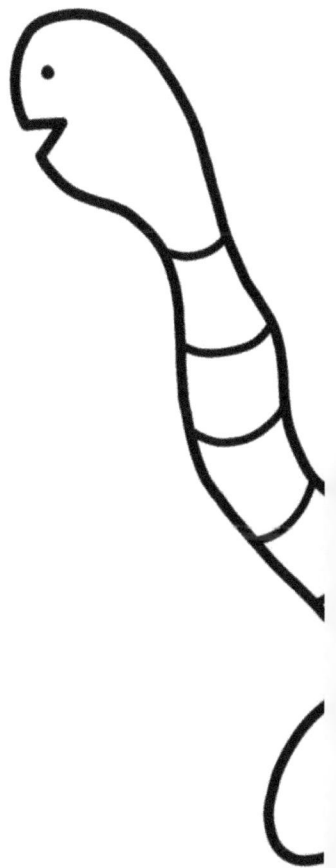
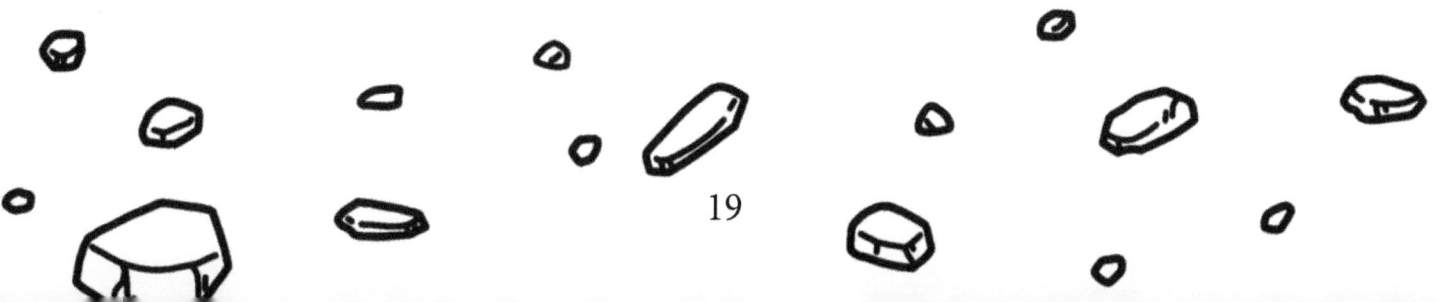

Embarrassed, she sunk back into the darkness.

The Worm went on his way.

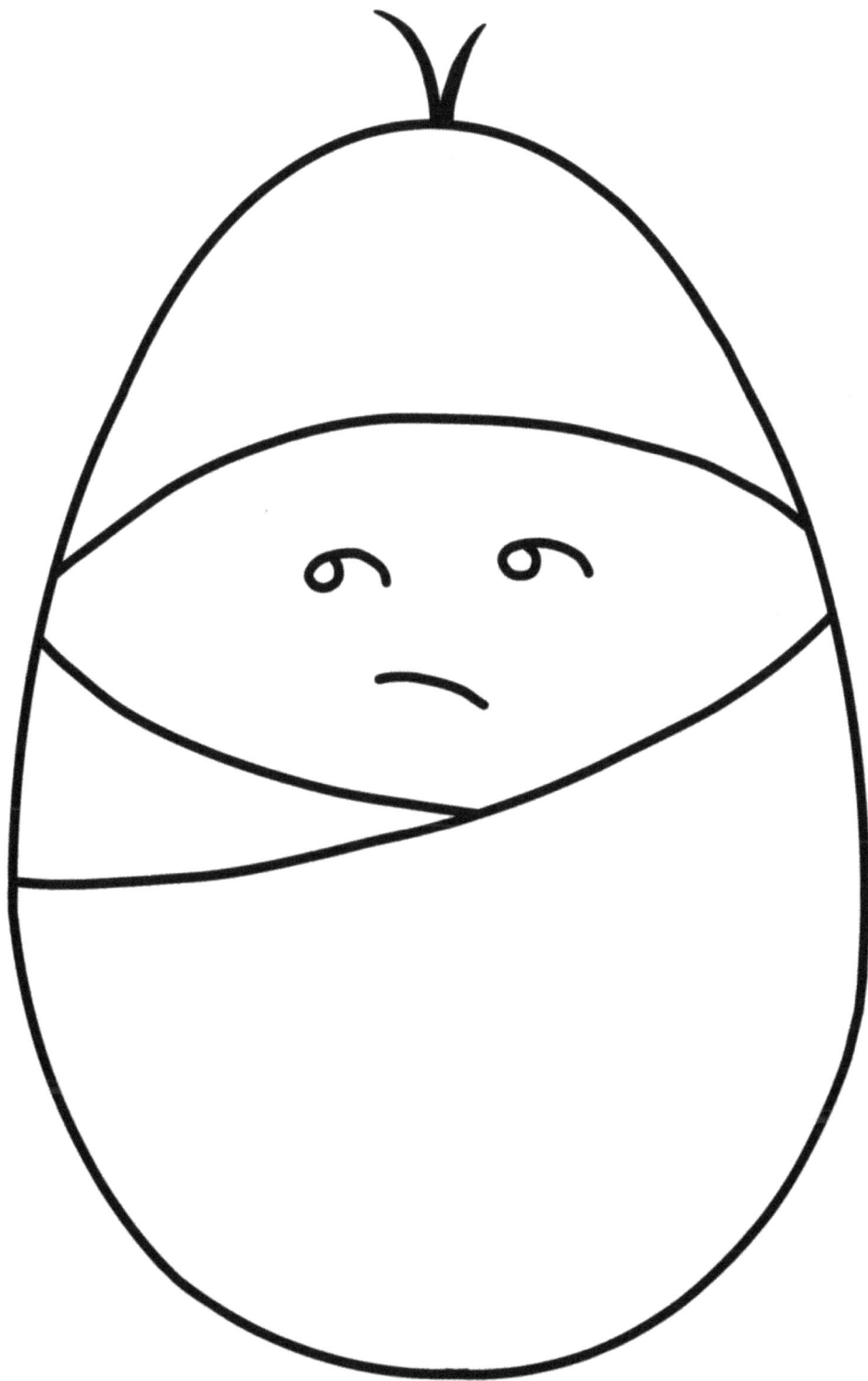

A few days later, The Worm wiggled his way

back to Little Seed again.

"Uggghhh. Please leave me alone", she sighed

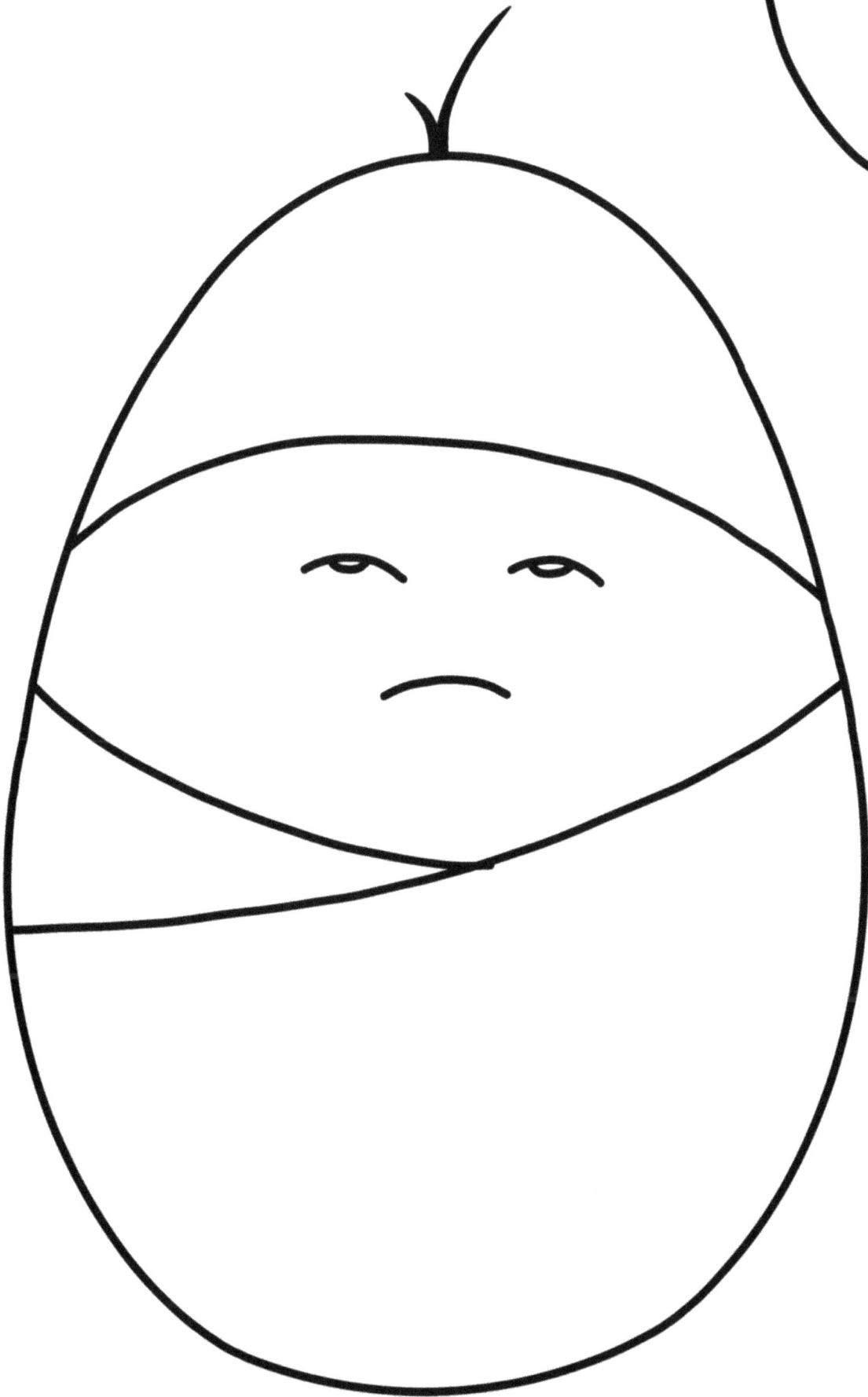

"I know how it feels to be alone."

"You do?" asked Little Seed.

"Yes, I didn't fit in either, but I learned that the only

thing that matters is how you feel about yourself."

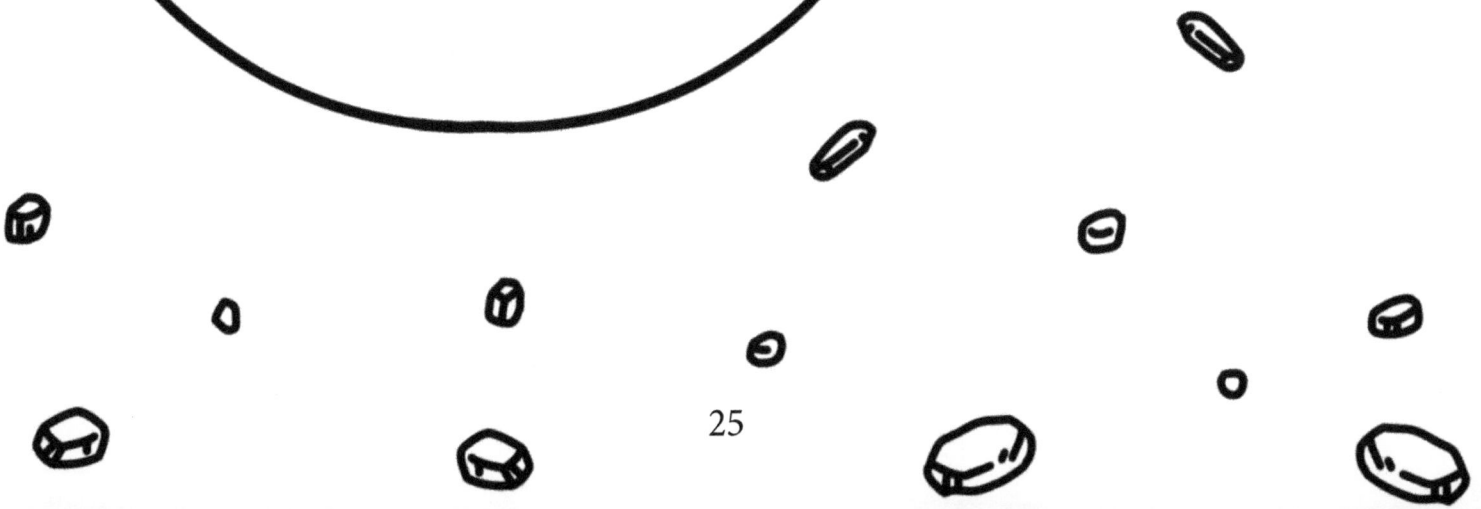

Little Seed pondered his words

and The Worm went on his way.

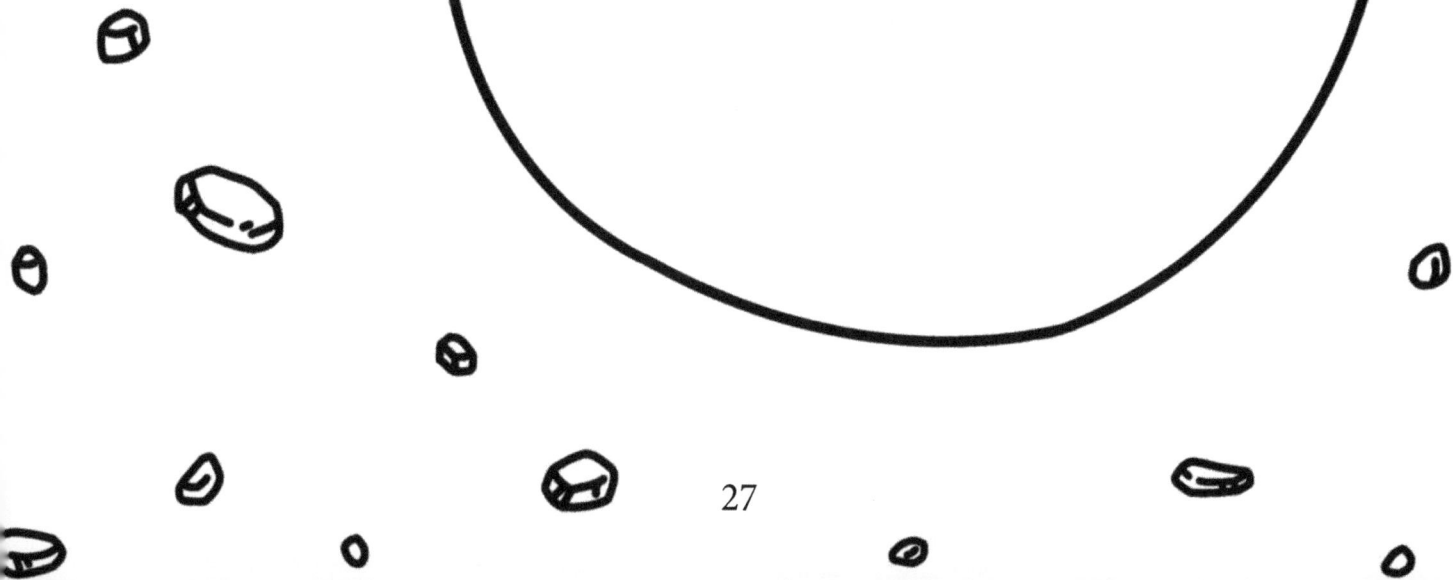

A few days passed and The Worm returned.

This time, Little Seed greeted him.

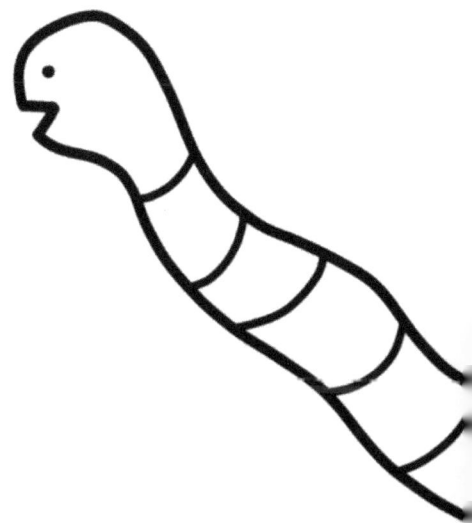

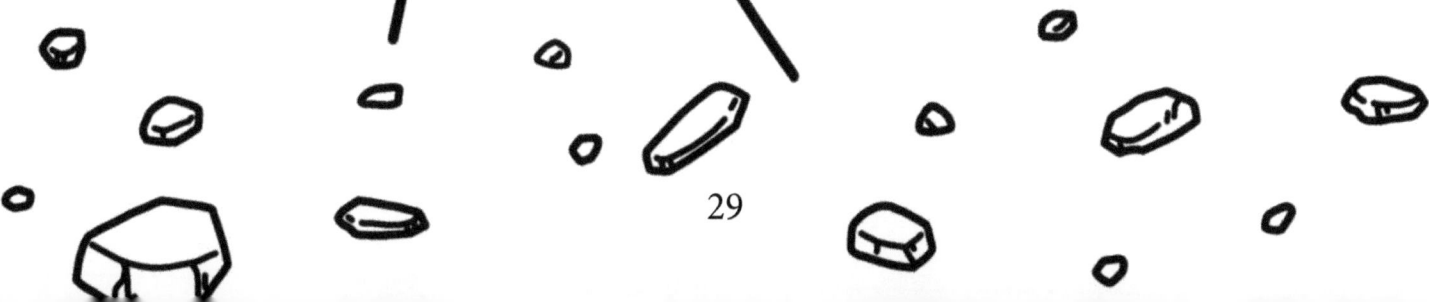

"I thought about what you said."

"You did?", The Worm inquired and leaned in.

"Remember how you said the only thing that matters

is how you feel about yourself?"

"Yes.", The Worm nodded.

Little Seed took a deep breath. "I don't feel good

about myself. How do I change that?"

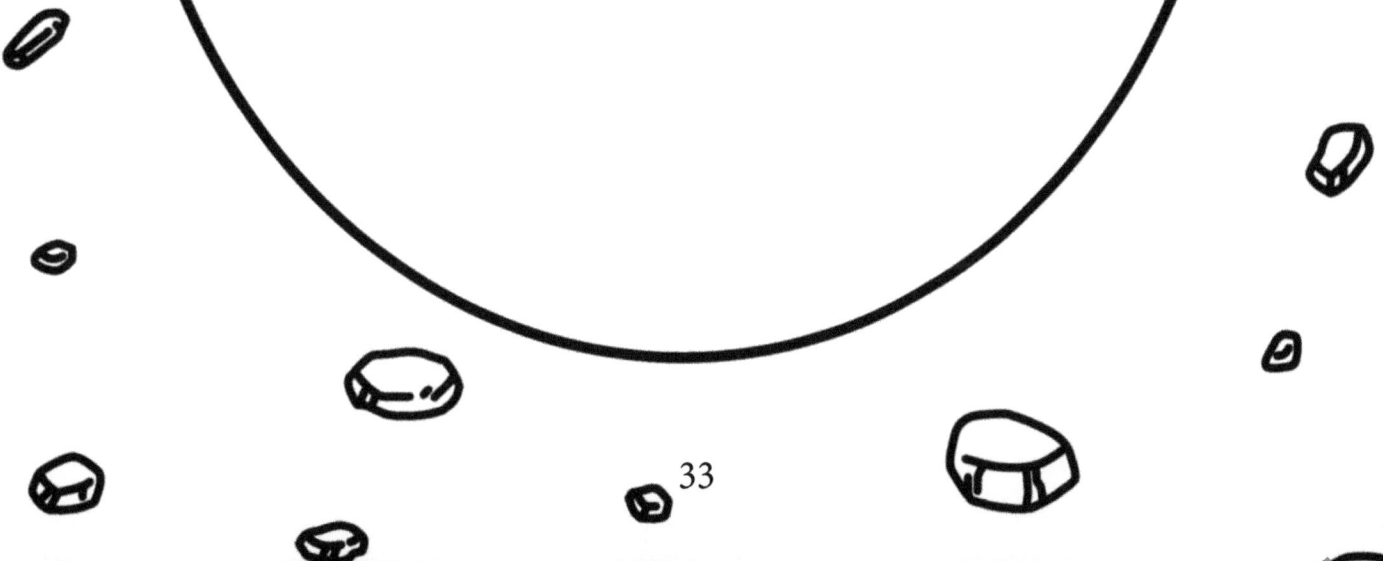

"With Love"

"Everyone has great qualities. Each day find one

thing that you like about yourself and

celebrate it all day long.", suggested The Worm.

"I like how colorful I am", Little Seed shared.

"That's a great start!"

Little Seed and The Worm danced around each

other in a budding friendship.

With The Worm by her side, she learned to love

herself in all of her beautiful ways.

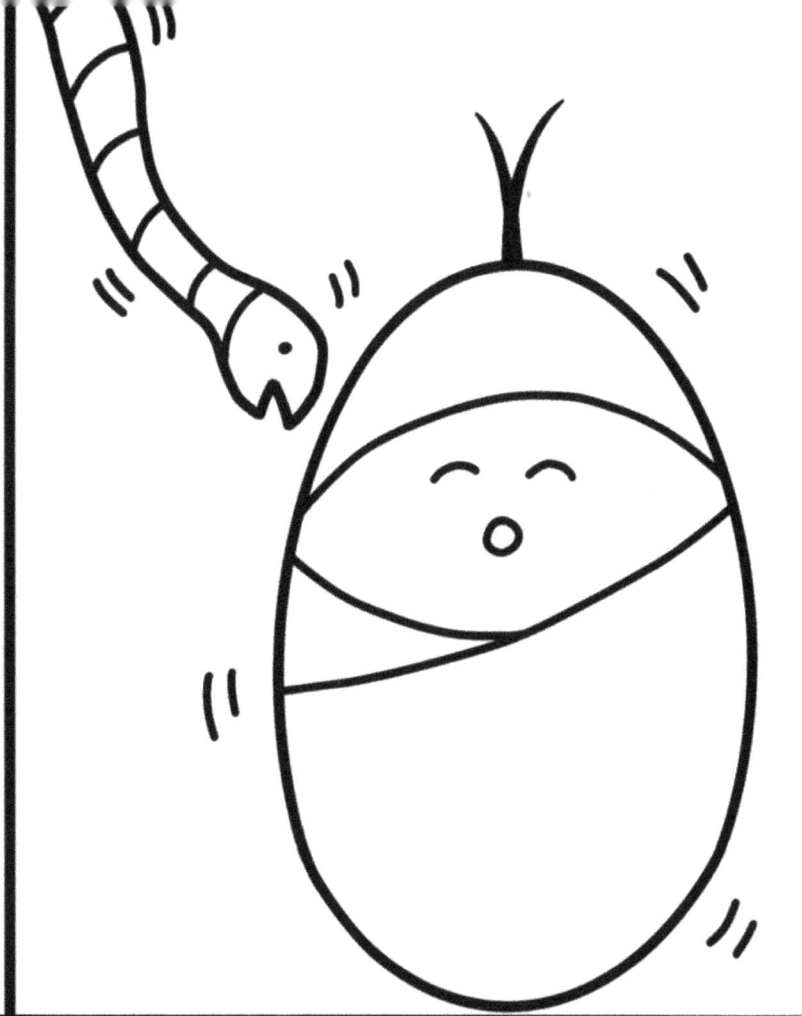

Little Seed found that she really did like herself.

With the sun's warmth shining upon her, she began

to open up and grow.

"I knew you could do it.", The Worm cried joyfully.

She kept growing and growing and growing until…

She became more than she ever imagined that she

could be.

She became a glorious tree!

For My Little Girl

US REVIEW OF BOOKS

"Yes, I didn't fit in either, but I learned that the only thing that matters is how you feel about yourself."

On the surface, Reynolds' children's book is vibrant and aesthetically pleasing. It captures the story of Little Seed, who rests peacefully on a branch until a storm plunges the seed to the forest floor, entirely outside of her comfort zone. When reality hits this lonely seed among a bunch of stranger seeds, she recedes inward, feeling shameful, leaving her to question her own identity.

The author subtly tackles one of the more relevant discussions among today's younger kids: creating divisions based on one's differences. As the other seeds make Little Seed feel like a misfit, The Worm gives Little Seed the realization that there is nothing more important than learning to love oneself. Affirmations and a positive mindset are central themes to Reynolds' work, helping tomorrow's adults unravel how to build confidence and self-esteem, all while examining one positive quality at a time.

The author's ability to create a simplified storytelling structure with easy, engaging characters to follow, chiefly Little Seed and The Worm, allows younger kids to invest themselves in the characters and attempt to model the actions of these characters in their own lives. Further, the writing style itself has a rhythmic cadence that feels more lyrical, even poetic, using elements of enjambment and repetition to create rhythm. Above all else, whether in the classroom, the library, or at the bedside, the author's children's book is well suited for younger kids beginning to understand their sense of self and learning to integrate themselves in an elementary school setting.

www.ingramcontent.com/pod-product-compliance
Lightning Source LLC
Chambersburg PA
CBHW042342030426

42335CB00030B/3437